Tommas's Story

Our Family is Broken ...

Lynley Barnett

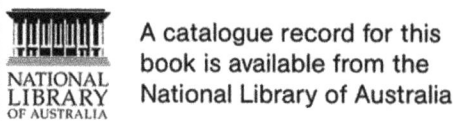 A catalogue record for this book is available from the National Library of Australia

Copyright Text: © 2023: Lynley Barnett
Copyright Illustrations: ©2023 Helen Iles
All rights reserved.
ISBN: 978-1-922727-92-3

Linellen Press
265 Boomerang Road
Oldbury, Western Australia
www.linellenpress.com.au

This is Tommas's story.

I am the eldest in the family.
I am fifteen. And this is a very unhappy time for us all.
Mum and Dad are getting a Divorce.

The worst part about our parents getting a divorce is that everyone expects me to help with the twins. They're ten and both girls. I have always helped with the girls but now I am constantly babysitting. And that means I don't get to see my own friends anymore.

When Mum and Dad told us they were buying another place and that Mum was going to live there, we were shocked.

Then they said that Dad was going to look after the girls while Mum went back to her career. Mum used to be an architect.

So suddenly she was gone. Dad has always been good at housework, not like a lot of dad's I know.

But Dad has a lot of other interests too and that's why I get lumbered with the babysitting.

We do have a routine for visiting Mum, and staying with her, and we know we can stay with her any other time so long as Dad agrees. He never says no but it is polite to ask him first.

So that we wouldn't be too confused Mum and Dad shared a lot with us.

They told us what they were going to do. And we did get to help choose furniture, and desks, and beds for Mum's new place.

What we do miss when we are at Mum's is the dog, Benji. He has to stay at Dad's because there is no garden for him at Mum's. He goes crazy when Mum pops around to see him. It's a pity dogs don't speak English because Benji has been very upset at Mum's leaving.

I think for a while we just did everything like always but every time I turned around to tell Mum something she wasn't there. And the girls speak another language altogether which Mum understood.

I know I am supposed to be manly and not to be sad, but I am. I don't want the girls to see me cry but I do sometimes. When they cry it is noisy and Dad is there to calm them. When I cry it is when I am on my own. I am just so sad that our family has broken up.

The girls have each other to talk to, but I didn't have anyone until my Grandpop spoke to me and told me being sad was OK. So I ride my bike to Pop's place on the weekends and he is always ready to talk to me.

I told my Pop that I was angry at Mum and Dad. It was like they didn't think about us, and I had always thought we were the most important people in their lives. But I see I was wrong. Pop really knows what I mean.

Mum wants to know if I mind if she sees another man. Just for coffee and perhaps a movie. I want her to be happy so I said OK. But I do mind really.

Mum is the one who helped me with my Maths assignments. It is so difficult now trying to make sense of some maths by myself.

Dad thought perhaps I could have a tutor, just to help before the exams. So I might do that.

The girls have got each other and I know that is good for them. But I only have Pop. My BF has shifted interstate, just when I really needed him.

I think part of the problem is that everything seemed to be ok, until it wasn't. And that has left me very confused. It's like I am studying, I see this girl who I like, I'm getting behind in my Maths, the girls get grumpy when I have to babysit and so do I, and everything hits me all at once.

And then to top it all off, the Coach of our Basketball team has been at me for missing practice. I just walked home after school thinking about so many things I completely forgot it was Basketball prac day. I have never done that before and he gave me a bollocking.

Something I really want to talk over with Mum and Dad is that I want to learn to make Robots. Our class at school has been talking with another school about joining our Robot programmes. This is something I could be good at, and there is this boy who has the same ideas as me, and we want to get together. We even said if it all worked out we would go into business together, but we know that will be a few years down the track. But right now, how can I get together with Jye (the boy from the other school) when Dad always wants me to babysit.

I don't want to babysit. How do I tell Dad that? He'll think I am being mean and unhelpful. I've thought about this for a long time and now I think I might ask Pop to help me. Perhaps he could talk to Dad for me. And maybe he could ask Dad to think about paying me, because every time I babysit Dad thinks it should be done for love.

And the other thing is who walks Benji? Me. That has also become my chore. The girls are old enough to walk the dog after school. They would be together so they wouldn't come to any harm, and they would only have to take him to the park around the corner. That's Benji's favourite place.

I don't know but it feels like I have taken over the Dad role in this house. I want to make friends with Jye, I want to practise basketball, and I want a tutor for my maths. Is that asking too much?

Am I being selfish? Do all kids who live in divorced homes have to do these kinds of chores? I really just want to be me. I want to find all the things I might be good at, and I want to have some fun too.

I told Pop he was like the Dali Lama - we learnt about him in school the other day - full of wisdom and always available to talk to. He smiled at that and said he thought we were just two good friends who hung out together. He likes using all the modern language.

So now I have to get used to the fact that my parents are almost divorced. And that is hard on the girls and me.

I am trying not to be angry or sad, but I do wish it hadn't happened. Didn't they realise that divorcing would upset my life and the girls'?

About the Author

Lynley Barnett spent many years working in Perth WA as an A.D.R.P. (Alternate Dispute Resolution Practitioner) or Mediator to you. She worked thousands of hours in Mediation, with adults, couples, and businesses.

She wrote this book to help children whose parents are divorced or divorcing.

www.ingramcontent.com/pod-product-compliance
Lightning Source LLC
Chambersburg PA
CBHW051350110526
44591CB00025B/2957